SARA TELLS THE TRUTH

Dalia Ramzi Mohammad

Editor: Noor Hammoud

"Gooaaal!" Sara cheered
as she kicked the ball into the goal.

She loved playing soccer.

She swerved right and left
as she dribbled the ball between her feet.

She kicked the ball so hard
that it flew above the goal
and into the garage.

As she ran to grab it,
there was a delicious smell
coming from inside the house.
When she walked in,
she was delighted to find fresh cookies!
She gobbled one up
as she ran back to her ball.
She brought it inside and began
to push the ball with her foot.

She remembered her mom's rule:

no balls in the house.

She thought to herself,

"It's okay, just this one time."

She kicked the ball

and it hit her mom's vase.

"Crash!" It broke into pieces.

"Oh no!" Sara shrieked.

She quickly cleaned up the mess.

Just then, her mom walked in.

"Sara, did you eat the cookies
I baked for you?" she asked.

"Yes I did, thank you Mama," Sara replied.

Her mom noticed the vase was missing.

She asked,

"Do you know what happened to my vase?"

Sara felt nervous.

She did not want her mom to get upset.

"No, I don't." Sara lied.

"Okay," her mom replied.

Sara went up to her room.

She felt horrible.

She did not follow the rules,

she broke her mom's vase,

and she lied.

Then she remembered how Allah

loves for us to tell the truth,

even if we are nervous.

She said, "Oh Allah, please forgive me."

Then she ran downstairs.

"Mama," Sara said,

"I have something to tell you."

"Yes, Sara?" her mom replied.

"I want to tell you the truth.

I played with my ball inside the house

and accidentally broke your vase.

I'm sorry," Sara confessed.

Her mom smiled and gave her a hug.

"Thank you for telling me the truth,"

her mom replied,

"I was sad about my vase,

but now you made me happy by being honest.

It's okay, mistakes happen and we learn from them.

What's important is that we always tell the truth."

Sara felt much better.

She then asked, "Mama, can I have another cookie?"

"Sure!" her mom replied.

They both smiled and ate their cookies together.

Dedicated to my hearts:

Moumen, Layla, Omar & Lena.

Sincere gratitude to my supportive father,

Ramzi Mohammad. I love you Baba.